Contents

Bible Baddies

BOB HARTMAN

Illustrations by Ron Tiner

LION
Children's Books

Text copyright © 1999 Bob Hartman
Illustrations copyright © 1999 Ron Tiner
This edition copyright © 2000 Lion Publishing

The moral rights of the author and illustrator
have been asserted

Published by
Lion Publishing plc
Sandy Lane West, Oxford, England
www.lion-publishing.co.uk
ISBN 0 7459 4212 1

First edition 1999
First paperback edition 2000
10 9 8 7 6 5 4 3 2 1 0

A catalogue record for this book is available
from the British Library

Typeset in 11.5/14 Baskerville BT
Printed and bound in Great Britain by
Omnia Books Ltd, Glasgow

Introduction

When most people think about the Bible it's the 'good guys' who come to mind. Noah and the ark. Daniel in the lions' den. Mary and Joseph and Jesus.

So why did I choose to write a book about Bible 'baddies'?

I suppose the first reason has to do with the fact that, as far as I could tell, no one had ever done it before! But there is another reason. You see, ever since I was a boy, going along to Sunday school with my parents, I have found the Bible baddies to be fascinating. Every story needs a villain, after all. And the stories in the Bible feature some of the most interesting villains of all time.

Some of them—vicious Eglon and ruthless Herod—are just downright evil. Others are sad and tragic, like proud Pharaoh and bitter Gehazi. Their stories are adventures, thrillers, mysteries—as powerful and exciting as tales you will read anywhere. And I hope that you will cheer when they get their comeuppance or are haunted by the evil they have set in motion.

But there are other villains you will meet in this book who are more interesting still. Oh, they're baddies, all right—murderers and thieves, cowards and cheats. But something happens during the course of their stories (something I wouldn't dream of giving away here!), and in the end, they are no longer baddies at all.

It's a kind of mystery, I suppose—maybe the most amazing mystery of them all. It's what makes these Bible baddies so fascinating. It's what made me want to write about them. And I hope it makes you want to read about them too!

Bob Hartman

The Tyrant's Tale

●　●　●　●　●　●　●　●　●　●　●　●

THE STORY OF PHARAOH

I've never liked the story of Pharaoh very much. Perhaps it has something to do with the fact that I'm the oldest of all my brothers and sisters, so that the last of the ten plagues—the killing of the first born—has always given me goosebumps. I can remember sitting in Sunday school, looking around the room and thinking, 'Yes, you would have been history, Andy Johnson. And you, too, Billy Holmes. And me too, of course!'

I was both glad that we didn't live in Egypt at the time of Moses and the Exodus, and angry that someone would put his own family at risk just to save his authority and his power. But that's what Pharaoh did. And that's how his story found its way into this book.

At first it was almost amusing.

'Did you see those two old men?' Pharaoh chuckled to

his magicians. 'They looked like a couple of goats, dragged out of the desert.'

'Desert goats!' agreed the first magician.

'Moses and A-a-a-ron,' baa-ed the second.

Pharaoh laughed out loud. 'And did you hear what they wanted?'

'LET MY PEOPLE GO!' mocked the first magician in a deep and booming voice.

'OR YOU'LL BE IN BIG TROUBLE!' boomed the second.

'THE GOD OF THE HEBREWS DEMANDS IT!' boomed Pharaoh, too. And they all laughed together.

Pharaoh wiped his eyes. 'I suppose I should cut off their heads,' he chuckled. 'But everyone needs a good laugh, now and then. And I've got to admit it: two desert tramps demanding that I, the supreme ruler of all Egypt, release some stupid Hebrew slaves is the funniest thing I've heard in a long time!'

'Ridiculous!' agreed the first magician.

'The craziest thing I ever heard!' added the second.

No one was laughing the next day, however, when Moses and Aaron walked up to Pharaoh as he strolled along the River Nile.

'Not you again!' Pharaoh sighed.

And his two magicians sighed with him.

'The Lord God has sent us,' Aaron explained. 'You refused to let his people go and so now, by his power, I will turn the waters of Egypt to blood!'

The magicians couldn't help it. They grinned, they chuckled, they burst into laughter. But when Aaron touched his staff to the river, the smiles dropped from their faces, for the water was blood-red.

'How did he do that?' Pharaoh whispered to his magicians.

'It's a… a… trick,' stuttered the first magician.

'A-anyone can do it,' explained the second.

'Then show me,' Pharaoh growled.

The magicians hurried off and managed to find a bowl of clear water. Then they walked slowly back to their master, careful not to spill a single drop. They said their secret words. They shook their sacred sticks. And the water in the bowl turned to blood, as well.

'See,' said a more confident Pharaoh to Moses and Aaron. 'Anyone can do it!'

'Anyone,' agreed the first magician, with a relieved sigh.

'Anyone at all!' proclaimed the second.

'And so,' Pharaoh concluded. 'You can tell your god that I will not let his people go.'

Seven days later, however, Moses and Aaron came to visit Pharaoh once again.

'This is starting to annoy me,' he muttered.

'And me, as well,' agreed the first magician.

'Peeved, that's what I am,' added magician number two.

But all Aaron said was, 'Frogs.'

'Frogs?' repeated a puzzled Pharaoh.

'Frogs?' echoed his two magicians.

'Frogs,' said Aaron, once again. 'Because you would not let his people go, our God will send frogs. Frogs in your houses. Frogs in your streets. Frogs all over your land.' And with that, Aaron waved his staff over the Nile and walked away.

Pharaoh glanced around. 'I don't see any frogs,' he grunted.

'No frogs here,' shrugged the first magician.

But the second magician simply said, 'Ribbit.'

'That's not funny,' Pharaoh growled.

'It wasn't me—honest,' the second magician pleaded. Then he lifted up his robe and pointed to his feet. 'It was him!'

The frog hopped slowly away. And then, all at once, an army of frogs poured out of the Nile to join him.

Pharaoh and his magicians ran as fast as they could— away from the river, away from the frogs. But when they hurried into the palace they realized there was no escape: the frogs were everywhere. Frogs on the floor, frogs on the furniture, frogs in the cups and plates and bowls!

'A simple trick,' panted the first magician.

'We can make frogs, too,' added the second.

'I'm so pleased to hear it,' Pharaoh grumbled. 'But can you make them go away?'

The magicians looked at one another, and then sadly shook their heads.

'Then fetch me Moses and Aaron,' Pharaoh sighed. 'I think it's time to give them what they want.'

So Pharaoh told Moses and Aaron that he would set the Hebrews—God's chosen people—free. Aaron smiled and raised his staff and the frogs all died.

But once they were gone, Pharaoh went back on his word and refused to let the Hebrews go.

So that is why the plagues continued, each one worse than the one before. And that is also why the magicians came to Pharaoh, at last, with a message they knew he would not want to hear.

'Your Majesty,' the first magician began, 'these plagues can only be the work of some very powerful god. You must stop the suffering. You must let the Hebrews go.'

'First there were the gnats,' moaned the second

magician. 'In our eyes and in our ears and up our noses!'

'And then there were the flies,' added the first magician. 'In our food and in our clothes and in our beds.'

'And then the animals died,' sniffled the second magician. 'The camels and the horses and the cows.'

'And now, these boils!' groaned the first magician.

'Stop your whinging!' shouted Pharaoh, as he struggled to his feet. 'Do you think that I am blind? That my family and I have not suffered as well? We, too, have swatted gnats and flies. We, too, have watched our animals die. And we, too, are now covered with these crippling sores. But if you think for a minute that I am going to give in to the Hebrews and their god, then you can think again. For I am Pharaoh, King of all Egypt, and no one—no one in heaven and no one on earth—is going to tell me what to do!'

And so the plagues continued.

Hail rained down on Pharaoh's fields and crushed all Egypt's crops. Then anything left growing was devoured by hungry locusts. Finally, darkness covered the whole of the land. And when the magicians had grown tired of bumping into the furniture and having nothing to eat, they took their empty stomachs and their skinned knees one last time into Pharaoh's palace.

They found him sitting—alone. He was no longer frustrated, no longer annoyed. No longer angry, no longer enraged. No, he just sat there, quietly brooding, with his teeth clenched tight and his knuckles white around the arm of his throne.

'What do you want?' he muttered, barely looking at his magicians.

'We want you to give up,' urged the first magician.

'Please!' begged the second. 'Please let the Hebrews go!'

'No one will think less of you,' the first magician argued. 'You have done all you could.'

'But the Hebrew god is just too strong!' added the second. 'And besides, we have heard. We have heard what the next plague will be.'

Pharaoh slowly raised his eyes and stared at his magicians. 'The death of the first-born,' he said softly. 'Your son, and your son,' he pointed. 'And mine as well.'

'Please, Your Majesty,' the first magician pleaded. 'My wife and I—we could not think of losing him!'

'We love our sons. And we know you love yours,' the second magician continued. 'And you have the power to save their lives!'

'Power?' sighed Pharaoh. 'What power? The god of the Hebrews controls the wind and the rain and the light. But I am just a king. And yet. And yet...' And here the king smiled a hard and cruel smile. 'And yet there is still one power that remains. The power to say "No".'

'But the children,' the magicians pleaded. 'The children will die!'

The king's smile turned into a hard and cruel stare. 'Sometimes,' he answered coldly, 'a leader has to harden his heart to the sufferings of his people for the sake of his people's good.'

'For his people's good,' sighed the first magician.

'Or for the sake of his own pride,' muttered the second magician.

'Out!' Pharaoh commanded. 'Get out!' he shouted again. 'And if you want to keep your heads, you will never return to this place!'

One week later, the magicians stood solemnly together and stared out over the Red Sea.

'So he let them go, after all,' the first magician sighed.

'The weeping. The wailing,' sighed the second magician in return. 'They say he tried hard to shut it out. But then his own son died—and that was too much, even for him.'

'So he let them go. And then he changed his mind—again!'

'I suppose he thought he had them trapped. Perhaps it never occurred to him that a god who could send locusts and hail and turn the Nile to blood could quite easily divide a sea, as well.'

'And so the Hebrews crossed on dry ground. And our own army? What about the soldiers sent after them?'

'Drowned. Drowned as they tried to follow. Drowned as the divided sea washed back over them.'

'So our suffering was for...'

'Nothing. Nothing at all.'

'And what about Pharaoh?' asked the first magician. 'What do you hear of him?'

The second magician shook his head. 'One of his servants told me that he has forbidden anyone in the palace to even speak about this event. And he has ordered the court historians to make no record of it whatsoever.'

'A proud man,' muttered the first magician.

'Proud to the end,' agreed the second.

And the two magicians turned away from the sea and walked sadly home.

The Avenger's Tale

• • • • • • • • • • • • • •

THE STORY OF EHUD AND EGLON

When I was a boy, I never tired of hearing the tale of Eglon and Ehud. It was full of blood and violence and gore—a long way removed from all that stuff about gentleness and love that we usually heard at church on a Sunday morning. But as I got older (and developed a deeper appreciation for that love and gentleness stuff), Eglon and Ehud became a little more troubling, along with a lot of the other Old Testament battle stories. And that's why I chose to include it in this collection.

I admit that I've done a lot of imagining and reading between the lines in this retelling. And I've added a few things you won't find in the Bible. But I have also tried to be true to what facts the Bible does give us. Eglon is still a wicked tyrant—an oppressor of the people of Israel. And Ehud is still *one of God's 'judges', chosen to rescue God's people in a time of crisis—chosen to kill King Eglon. But even in the most 'just' cases, surely, killing has its repercussions. And that is what this story is about.*

Every night it was the same. For eighteen years, the same. Ehud would wake up, suddenly, cold and sweating and afraid. And that face, the face in the dream, would be laughing at him all over again.

Shouting, that's how the dream began.

'The Moabites are coming! They've crossed the river and they're heading towards the village!'

What followed next was a mad, rushing blur—a spinning haze of colour and fear and sound. His father's hand. His sister's screams. His mother's long black hair. Goats and pots and tables, running and flying and falling down.

And then, suddenly, everything would slow down again, to half its normal speed. And that's when the man would appear. The laughing man. The fat man. Eglon, King of Moab.

He would climb down from his horse, every bit of his big body wobbling. And with his soldiers all around, hacking and slicing and killing, he would walk up to Ehud's family, each step beating in time with the little boy's heart.

His father, Gera, would fall to his knees. His mother, as well, with his sister in her arms. And then the big man, laughing still, would raise his sword and plunge it first into his father, and then through his mother and his sister, too.

Finally, the laughing man would raise his bloodied sword and turn to Ehud, five-year-old Ehud. But before the king could strike, there would come a sound, a call, from somewhere off in the distance. The king would turn his head, look away for just a second, and Ehud would start to run—run between the burning buildings, run past his dying neighbours, run until the nightmare was over, run... until he awoke.

Every night, for eighteen years—that's how long the dream had haunted Ehud. But tonight, he promised himself, tonight the dream would come to an end. For today, King Eglon of Moab, the fat man, the laughing man, the man who had murdered Ehud's family, would come to an end, as well.

Ehud thanked God for his family, and particularly for his father, and the gift that his father had passed on to him. It was a gift that not even the Moabites could take away, a gift that made him the perfect candidate for the job he was about to do—the gift of a good left hand.

Most soldiers were right-handed. They wore their swords hanging from the left side of the body and reached across the body to draw them from their sheaths. That was what the enemy looked for, that was what the enemy watched—the right hand. For the slightest twitch, the smallest movement of that hand might signal that a fight was about to begin. So, a left-handed man enjoyed a certain advantage, particularly if his sword was hidden.

Ehud rubbed his eyes, rolled off his sleeping mat and reached for his sword—the special sword that he had designed just for this mission.

It was only eighteen inches long, far too short for battle, but just the right size for strapping to his thigh and hiding under his robes. And it was sharpened on both edges so he could cut in both directions. He'd wipe the smile from the fat man's face, all right—even if he had to slice it off!

He'd waited for this day for eighteen years. And for

those same eighteen years, the nation of Israel had been paying tribute to King Eglon. For the invasion which had destroyed Ehud's village had also swept across the land and resulted in Israel's surrender to Moab. And so, every year, great quantities of treasure and produce and livestock had to be delivered to the royal palace and presented to Eglon himself, as a sign of Israel's submission.

Today was the day—Tribute Day. And the man chosen to lead Israel's procession, chosen by God himself to walk right into the presence of the king, was none other than Ehud, the left-handed man, the man with the sword strapped to his thigh, the man who was finally in a position to set both himself and his people free.

Ehud thought he would be nervous, but instead he was overcome with a sense of calm and purpose. He led the procession, according to plan, out of Israel and across the Jordan river, past the stone statues of Gilgal and into the palace of the king.

He had imagined this moment for years—face to face, finally, with the man he hated most in all the world. 'What will I feel?' he had often wondered. 'Hatred? Disgust? The overwhelming urge to reach out and strike Eglon where he stands?' All those feelings, he knew, had to be overcome if the plan was to succeed. He had to be submissive, polite and reverential if he was to win the trust of this tyrant. But when Eglon at last appeared, Ehud was shocked by what he actually felt.

The king was still a big man—now far heavier than Ehud had remembered. So heavy, in fact, that his attendants had to help support his weight as he staggered toward his throne. And as for laughter, there was none at all, not even a chuckle—just a hard and constant wheeze as the man struggled to move.

Pity. That's what Ehud felt. And he couldn't believe it. Pity and the surprising sense that, somehow, he had been robbed. This was not the man he'd dreamed of—the fat man, the laughing man, the nightmare man. No, this was a sad and pathetic man, crippled by excess and by power and unable to raise a sword even if he had wanted to.

Still, Ehud reminded himself, there was the mission—the job he believed God had sent him to do. And pity or not, for the sake of his people, he would do it.

And so he bowed and he scraped and he uttered the obligatory words:

'Noble Potentate, Ruler of all you survey, Great and Mighty One.'

Then he stepped aside as, one by one, the gifts were laid before the king. Eglon, however, hardly paid attention. He nodded, almost imperceptibly, and acknowledged each part of the tribute with the slightest wave of his hand. It looked to Ehud as if he was bored with the whole affair, or just too old and tired to care.

When the formalities had finished, Ehud sent his entourage away, then turned to the king and said, 'I have a secret message for you, Your Majesty.'

For the first time, Eglon looked interested. His dull eyes showed some spark of life as they focused on Ehud.

'Silence!' the king wheezed at his attendants. 'This man has something to tell me.'

Ehud looked around, nervously. 'It's for your ears only,' he whispered. 'Perhaps if we could meet somewhere… alone?'

The king considered this, and then nodded. 'Very well,' he agreed. 'Meet me upstairs, in my roof chamber. It's cooler there, anyway. Oh,' and here he glanced at the sword that hung from Ehud's side, the long sword, the decoy

sword, 'you will, of course, leave your weapon outside.'

Ehud smiled and bowed, 'Of course!'

That smile never left Ehud's face—not once, while he waited for the king to be helped up to his chamber. For the plan was working perfectly, as all the spies had said it would.

Eglon loved secrets, they had assured him. Dealing and double-dealing, they explained, was how he had hung onto his throne. And that made this plan all the more sweet. For Ehud's robe concealed a secret that the king would never expect!

Finally, the guards called Ehud up to the roof chamber. They looked at him suspiciously. They took away the sword that hung at his side. Then they sent him in to the king.

Ehud bowed again. And the king waved him forward.

'So who is this message from?' asked Eglon, and the cruelly calculating look in his eyes reminded Ehud, at last, of the man he saw each night in his dreams.

'From one of your commanders?' the king continued. 'Or from one of your spies? Or perhaps the sight of all that treasure has convinced you to speak for yourself—to betray your own people?' And with that, the king began to laugh. A little, choked and wheezing laugh, but it was enough—enough to rekindle Ehud's ebbing wrath, enough to force him to play his secret hand.

'No,' he answered firmly. 'The message is not mine nor my commanders'. The message I have for you is from God himself.' And he reached his left hand under his robe and drew his sword.

Three times—that was how he had always planned it. Once for his father, once for his mother, once for his poor murdered sister. But the first blow was so fierce, that the sword plunged all the way in, swallowed up past its hilt in fatty folds of Eglon's stomach. And even though Ehud tried to retrieve it, all he got was a fistful of entrails and blood.

Ehud locked the chamber doors to buy himself some time, then he hurried out down the servants' staircase. A part of him wanted to savour this moment—to stand and gloat over Eglon's bloated corpse. But if he was to avoid a similar fate, he needed to run. And he thanked God for the escape route the spies had plotted out for him.

Down from the roof chamber and along the quiet corridors of the private quarters—that was the plan. And, sure enough, he passed no one but a startled maid. He rehearsed it as he went: one more turn, one more hallway, and he would be out. But as he dashed around the final corner, he stumbled over something and fell in a sprawling heap onto the floor.

It was a boy. A little boy. 'He's not hurt,' thought Ehud with relief.

'Who are you?' the little boy asked, as he picked himself up and flashed a friendly smile.

'I'm... umm... it's not important,' Ehud stammered. 'I have to be going.'

'Well, if you see my grandfather,' the boy said, 'will you tell him I'm looking for him? He said he would tell me a story.'

'Your grandfather?' asked Ehud.

'The king, silly!' the little boy grinned. 'Everybody knows that!' And Ehud just stood there, frozen.

He could hear the chamber doors crashing down. He could hear the shouts of the attendants, and their cries, 'The king, the king is dead! Someone has murdered the king!'

He had to go. He had so little time. But all he could do was stand there. And look at the boy. And look at his own bloodied hand. And look at the boy again. And watch as the smile evaporated from his innocent five-year-old face.

And then Ehud ran. Ran as he ran in his dream. Out of the palace and past the stone statues to the hills of Seirah. The army of Israel was waiting there—waiting for his return. And as soon as he shouted, 'King Eglon is dead!', the army swooped down to the valley below.

Ten thousand died that day. Moab was defeated. Israel was freed. And Ehud had his revenge, at last. And, after much carousing and shouting and celebrating, he rolled, exhausted, onto his mat, looking forward to his first full night's sleep in eighteen years.

But unlike Ehud's enemies, the dream would not be so easily defeated. For as the night wore on, it returned—more real than ever.

There was the little boy. There was the shouting. There was the slashing and the screaming and the dying... Ehud trembled and shook, just as he had done for eighteen years. But when he looked, at last, into the eyes of the man with the bloodied sword, Ehud awoke with a start. For the man with the sword was left-handed. And the killer's face was his own.

The Murderer's Tale

● ● ● ● ● ● ● ● ● ● ● ● ●

THE STORY OF DAVID

When I was a kid, I always wanted to know—who were the 'good guys', and who were the 'bad guys'? I guess that's why I found the story of David and Bathsheba so confusing. As far as I could tell, David was one of the good guys. He defeated the evil giant, Goliath. He escaped the murderous pursuit of King Saul. And he became the greatest ruler that Israel ever had.

And yet, there was that other story. The one about the naked lady on the rooftop who caught David's eye. The one we always giggled at in our Sunday school class. The one where David wasn't such a good guy after all.

What's the difference between the good guys and the bad guys? Maybe it has to do with the choices people make once they've done something wrong. Ignoring wrongdoing, *or explaining it away, or trying to act as if it was a good thing, seems to make them badder still. But when they admit that they have been wrong, and give God the chance to do something about it, he makes it possible for them to be good guys again. Even when they've stumbled just as far as David had. Yes, even David, the one the Bible calls, 'a man after God's own heart'.*

It was like walking down the stairs. The first step was easy, so easy that he hardly noticed his feet had moved. He saw her. He fancied her. He wanted her. It was as simple as that and more complicated than his passion would allow. For he was the King of Israel. And she was another man's wife.

There must have been some part of him willing to admit that this was wrong. But her lips, and her skin, and her soft falling fountain of hair covered him and consumed him and chased away every other care. And the most he could remember thinking was that God 'owed him one'.

He'd killed the giant, after all. And united the kingdom. And repaid the cruelty of his predecessor, Saul, with kindness and patience and respect.

He was David, God's chosen and anointed king. David, faithful and trusting and true. Surely, he thought, this little indiscretion, this passing moment of passion, could do no long-term harm.

It was like walking down the stairs. But, suddenly, they were narrow and steep and uneven. And the second step proved much harder than the first.

'I'm pregnant,' explained Bathsheba. 'And there is no question about it. The child is yours.'

Of course it was his. Her husband, Uriah, was away at

war. Fighting David's war. But there was still time to avoid a scandal. And a way to do it, as well. It would involve a little deception, yes. But surely that was better than the humiliation of God's chosen king. So David called Uriah home from the front.

'You've fought hard!' David said. 'You've fought well!' And then, with a nod and a wink, he added, 'Spend tonight at home with your wife. It's the least you deserve.'

Uriah left the king. But he did not go home. He lay down outside the king's palace, instead, with the rest of the king's servants. So when the morning came, David sent for him again.

'I meant what I said,' he explained. 'You've had a long journey. Go home, spend some time with your wife!'

'But how can I?' Uriah sighed. 'My commander Joab and all my fellow soldiers are camping out in the fields. How could I possibly enjoy myself when I should be doing my duty and sharing in their hardship? You're a soldier too, Your Majesty. I know you understand these things. And so I shall sleep outside again tonight.'

David kept on trying. He invited Uriah to stay in Jerusalem for two more days. He fed Uriah and he flattered Uriah and he gave him so much wine to drink that Uriah could barely stagger outside each night. But still Uriah would not go home. For he was a faithful soldier, more faithful than David had ever imagined.

And that's what made the third step so hard.

It was like walking down the stairs. But now those stairs were crumbling under David's feet, and it seemed as if there was nothing he could do but fall.

A scandal had to be avoided. There was no question about it. And, more than that, Bathsheba was no longer just a passing fling.

He hadn't managed to talk Uriah into sleeping with her, but he had convinced himself completely. She was beautiful. She was carrying his child. And he wanted her. Not just for an afternoon's entertainment—but for ever. And there was only one way to make that happen. He would have to take the final step—from adultery, to deceit... to murder.

He sent the letter by Uriah's own hand.

'Give this to your commander, Joab,' he ordered. 'It is for his eyes only.'

A lesser soldier, an unfaithful servant, might have read the letter, and in so doing, saved his life. But Uriah was a good man, so he delivered his own death warrant into Joab's hand.

'Put Uriah at the front,' the letter said, 'at the spot where the fighting is hardest. Then pull your men back—and leave him alone to die.'

Joab did what he was told. He had no reason to question his king's command. David wanted this man dead. Who was he to argue?

When the news reached Bathsheba, she wept. And when the time of mourning was over—the proper time, the respectable time—David took her into his palace and married her.

It was over. It was done with. David should have been happy. But he wasn't. Because he knew that what he'd done was just like walking down the stairs. And the stairs had led him to a dungeon.

Everywhere he looked, there was darkness.

Guilt shadowed his every move. Bright days seemed cloudy. Good friends seemed distant. And even the reports of victory from the battle front seemed hollow—for they reminded him of the face of only one fallen soldier.

As for Bathsheba, was it just his imagination, or the way the evening sun caught her eye? But he couldn't help feeling that she looked different, too. Did she know? Had she guessed? And would that suspicion—if that was even what it was—for ever come between them?

And God. The God who had defeated the giant and rescued David in the desert and given him his throne. God, his light and his salvation. Even God seemed dark and distant now.

What was wrong with all of them? He had done what he had to do, and now there was no way to undo it. All he could do was put things behind him and try to carry on. So that's what David did with his guilt and his sadness and his shame. He stuffed them deep down inside himself—as he'd once stuffed supplies into a bag and taken them to his

brothers, as he'd once stuffed five small stones into his hand.

The darkness, however, would not go away. The dungeon walls refused to disappear. So that's where he was sitting one day when the prophet, Nathan, came to call.

'I have a story to tell you,' Nathan announced. And David just sighed and waved for him to go on. The darkness was real. The dungeon walls were closing in. It was hard to see how a story could help.

'Make it quick,' David ordered. 'I have things… to think about.'

'Once upon a time,' Nathan began, 'there were two men. One was rich and the other poor. The rich man had more sheep than he could count, but the poor man had only one —a little ewe lamb which he cuddled and cared for and raised like one of his own children. He fed it from his table.

He let it drink from his mug. No lamb was ever loved more.'

David forced a weary smile. 'If only life were as sweet and simple as stories,' he thought.

'One day,' Nathan continued, 'the rich man had a visitor. He wanted to make this visitor a meal—the very best meal. But he wasn't keen to sacrifice any of his own lambs. So guess what he did? He went out and stole the poor man's lamb, and made a meal of it, instead.'

Something erupted inside David. His own guilt and anger exploded at the man in the story.

'Who is this man?' David shouted. 'Tell me his name and I promise you, he will be punished.'

The prophet looked at the king and then said very slowly, 'The man in the story... is you.'

Everything stopped for a second. It was as if David had been run through with a sword or slammed into a cold hard wall. And then, just as if he were sliding down the face of that wall, he dropped slowly to his knees.

Nathan knew. Of course, he knew. God had told him. And God had known all along.

'There will be a price to pay,' the prophet continued. 'Your family will be plagued with violence. Your wives will be unfaithful. And your child, the child that Bathsheba is carrying, will die.'

The tears came rushing out now, just as the anger had. 'I have sinned,' admitted David, at last. 'I and I alone have brought this pain upon the people I love.'

And with that admission, suddenly, there was light. It didn't make sense. There should have been darkness and more darkness still. But instead there was light. Not much light, but enough to see again, enough to make his way out of the dungeon.

And so David stood, weeping still.

'I'm sorry,' he said to Nathan.

'I'm sorry,' he said to God.

It was a small step, a feeble step, the first of many hard and painful steps. But it was a step towards the light. In fact, it was just like walking—walking back up the stairs.

The Con Man's Tale

• • • • • • • • • • • • • •

THE STORY OF GEHAZI

Many biblical characters lived up to the meaning of their names. Abraham became 'the father of a multitude'. Peter proved, in the end, to be a 'rock'. And Jesus was most definitely 'God's Saviour'.

Gehazi, on the other hand, managed to live down to his name. 'Belittler', 'diminisher', that's what 'Gehazi' means. And that's how he lived his life. He was a servant of the prophet Elisha and a witness to many miracles. But his response to at least one of those wonders was to reduce it to an opportunity for personal gain.

Next to the murder, oppression and betrayal you will find in the rest of this book, Gehazi's misdeeds don't seem so bad. Or, maybe it's just more common to take something beautiful and pure and turn it into something cheap and dirty *and insignificant. It's the trick of the gossip, the liar, the con man. And maybe, in the end, it's one of the most destructive kinds of badness of all.*

'That's right!' Gehazi boasted. 'I worked for Elisha: the Number One Servant to the Number One Prophet in all Israel!'

His companions shuffled closer to the fire, eager to hear what Gehazi had to say, yet careful for their numb fingers and toes. For they were lepers, every one of them.

'You must have seen some amazing things!' one leper whispered.

'Tell us about them,' begged another.

'Where does one begin?' Gehazi sighed. 'Particularly when one's stomach is complaining. I don't suppose... ?'

'Yes, yes of course!' said a third leper, handing him a piece of bread. 'Tell us your story and you can share our little meal.'

'But get on with it!' came a fourth voice, a muffled voice, from out of the darkness. 'We haven't got all night!'

'The woman from Shunem,' announced Gehazi through a mouthful of bread. 'That is where we will begin!' Then he swallowed hard and cleared his throat. 'She was rich. I can tell you that, for a start.'

'And beautiful?' asked one of the lepers.

'Not my type,' Gehazi shrugged. 'And as for Elisha? Well, who can say? What I can tell you is that every time we passed through Shunem, we visited there. Just for meals, at first, but then she talked her husband—who was much older than her, by the way—into fixing up a little room for us. A bed, a lamp, a table. All mod cons!'

'A bed!' sighed one of the lepers.

'And a table!' sighed another.

'What can I say?' Gehazi bragged. 'Elisha's an important fellow. And don't let anybody fool you—this prophet thing is not *all* about pain and sacrifice. It's also got its fair share of fringe benefits!

'So, anyway, there we were, in the lap of luxury, so to speak, when we heard something. It was the lady. The rich lady. And she was downstairs, crying.

'Well, Elisha turned to me and he said, "What do you think is the matter?"

'Some prophet, eh? Asking *me*!' Gehazi sniggered. 'Anyway, I said the first thing that came into my head. Her husband was old. She had no children. Maybe that was the problem.

'Elisha nodded and thought about this for a minute. Then he told me to go and fetch her. Well, she stood there in the doorway, drying her eyes, and you're never going to believe what he told her.

' "A year from now..." he said, "a year from now you will be standing in that same doorway, holding a son in your arms!"

'I couldn't believe it! I mean, there we were, set up like kings: beds, tables, lamps, and three square meals a day! And he wanted to go and ruin it all! He got her hopes up. He got her all excited. But he never stopped to think—what if we showed up a year later, and there was no little boy in her arms? What then? No food to eat. No place to stay. That's what!'

And here Gehazi stopped.

'Well... what happened?' asked one of the lepers. 'Did she have the baby or not?'

Gehazi held up his hands. 'In a minute,' he gasped. 'I'm getting a little parched, here. I don't suppose there's any wine in that bag of yours?'

'Yes. Yes, of course,' said the lepers.

'And another piece of that bread would be nice,' Gehazi added.

'Well, it's all we've got, but...'

And before the leper could finish, Gehazi grabbed the bread from his hand. He swallowed the wine and he stuffed the bread in his mouth. But while he was still chewing, the man at the edge of the circle coughed.

'You were going to tell us what happened,' he said.

Gehazi nodded, chewed some more, and then after one last, large swallow, he answered. 'She had the child. Simple as that.'

'So it was a miracle!' marvelled one of the lepers.

'If you say so,' Gehazi shrugged. 'Or maybe it was just a happy coincidence. Who knows?' And then the fire caught a gleam, a nasty gleam, in Gehazi's eye.

'Or, maybe...' he suggested. 'Just maybe...' And then he stopped himself. 'No, I'd better not.'

'Tell us! Please tell us!' the lepers shouted. 'What do you think really happened?'

'Weell...' Gehazi leaned forward and whispered, 'I have no proof of this. It's all circumstantial. But Elisha would often send me off on long errands. And that meant, of course, that he was alone with the woman in the house!'

The lepers gasped, 'You don't mean... ?'

'Anything's possible,' Gehazi grinned.

The lepers nudged and sniggered and poked at each other. They'd never heard anything like this before!

'Tell us more!' they begged.

'Yes,' came the voice from the darkness, quieter now, and more intense. 'Tell us more.'

'Well, I'll have to have another drink,' Gehazi began, as he grabbed for the wine and nearly finished it. Then he

thought for a moment and said, 'The son. Why don't I tell you about the woman's son?

'It was years later. The boy was old enough to go and help the workers in the fields. Well, one day, he started complaining about headaches. "My head! My head!" he shouted. And he wouldn't stop. So one of the servants took him home. And later that day he died.'

'The poor boy!' moaned one of the lepers.

'And the poor mother, too,' moaned another.

'Can I go on?' asked Gehazi, annoyed at the interruption. 'Now we didn't know anything about this. We were up on Mount Carmel, at the time, when Elisha saw the boy's mother galloping towards us on one of her donkeys. She was riding him for all he was worth. It was obvious that something was wrong. I mean, rich ladies don't usually go tearing around on the backs of donkeys. So Elisha sent me down to see what she wanted.

' "How are you?" I asked. "How's your husband? How's the little boy?" Well, she mumbled something about everything being fine, but I knew it wasn't, of course, because she rode right past me as if I wasn't even there and headed straight for Elisha.

'I ran after her, and it was a good thing. Because as soon as she got to the top, she jumped off the donkey and went for Elisha. I grabbed her and I pulled her away. It was lucky for him that I was there. But then—well, you know how it is with these prophets—he did the strangest thing. He told me to let go of her.

' "There's something wrong here," he said. (No kidding! I thought.) But then he admitted that God hadn't told him what it was yet.

'Well, she told him. And you didn't have to be a prophet to understand it!

' "You lied to me!" she screamed. "You deceived me! You promised me a son and now your God has taken him away!"

'Then the whole story came pouring out and, in the middle of the weeping and the wailing, Elisha handed me his staff.

' "Go to the boy!" he ordered. "Don't stop to say hello to anybody. And if anybody says hello to you, walk right past him. Go to the boy and lay my staff on his face. Now!" '

Gehazi grimaced. 'He could be pushy like that, sometimes. Anyway, I went, and even though I'm sure I offended a friend or two, I didn't stop to talk to anyone. I went straight to the house and into the child's room. And he was just lying there...'

'Dead?' asked one of the lepers.

'I guess so,' Gehazi answered. 'I mean, I'd never seen a dead person before. He could have been sleeping for all I knew. But I did what Elisha told me. I laid the staff on his face.'

'And... ? Then what?' begged another leper.

'Nothing,' said Gehazi. 'Well, what did you expect? It's not as if the staff was magical or anything. It was just a big walking stick.'

'So what did Elisha do?' asked a third leper.

'I'm getting to that,' Gehazi assured him. 'But first I think I need another drink.'

'There are only a few drops left...' one of the lepers began.

'That'll do,' said Gehazi, and then he continued.

'Elisha showed up in a little while. The boy's mother was with him. She was still pretty hysterical and she said she wouldn't leave until he did something. So Elisha went into the boy's room and shut the door.

He told me later that he prayed. Then he laid himself on

top of the boy—eye to eye, mouth to mouth, hand to hand —until the boy's skin started to get warm. Then he walked around the room for a while. Finally, he lay close to the boy again. And that's when we heard the sneeze.'

'The sneeze?' asked one of the lepers.

'Well, seven sneezes, actually. Then we knew the boy was alive.'

'Another miracle!' exclaimed the lepers.

And again Gehazi just shrugged. 'Maybe. Or maybe I was right the first time. Maybe he was just sleeping or dazed or something. And maybe the weight of the prophet started to smother him, and he choked and that's what woke him up. That would explain the sneezing for sure.'

The voice from the darkness, the muffled voice, called out again. 'So what you're saying is that this Elisha never really performed any miracles at all—that he's some kind of phoney.'

'Your words, not mine,' Gehazi grinned. And then he added, just a little nervously, 'Why don't you come closer to the fire and join us, neighbour? It's warmer here, and there's plenty to eat.'

'No, I'm comfortable where I am,' the voice called back. 'I'm afraid my features would frighten you. And, besides, it looks like you've already gobbled everything up. I was wondering, though. Could you tell us the story of Naaman? Naaman the leper.'

'A leper? Oh, yes!' everyone else chimed in.

'Naaman?' mumbled Gehazi, more nervous still. 'I don't think I remember that one.'

A coin—a single silver coin—flew out of the darkness, catching the firelight as it flipped and spun and landed at Gehazi's feet.

'Perhaps this will remind you,' the voice called out. 'And

there is another, in my bag, when you have finished.'

Gehazi's anxiety battled with his greed. And in the end, greed won—as it always did.

'Naaman?' he began. 'Well, there's not much to say. Naaman was a Syrian—a commander in their army. And he was also a leper. A little Israelite slave girl who worked in his house, told him about Elisha. So he came to the prophet, offering Elisha a small fortune, if only the prophet would heal him. Elisha passed the message on through me—yes, I remember it now—and told Naaman to dip himself seven times in the Jordan river. Naaman did what Elisha told him, and when he came up the seventh time…'

'He was healed,' the voice from the darkness finished. 'Isn't that right, Gehazi?'

'Well, yes, but…'

'But, what?' the voice continued. 'The man was a leper —more disfigured than anyone around this fire. And when he did what Elisha told him, he was healed. What could you call that, but a miracle?'

For the first time, Gehazi was speechless. So one of the lepers spoke up, instead.

'It's just a shame, isn't it, Gehazi,' he said, 'that Elisha couldn't heal your leprosy, as well.'

'Yes it is,' agreed the voice from the darkness. 'But then you haven't told us, Gehazi, how you came to be a leper in the first place.'

Gehazi wrapped his rags around himself. 'Story-time is over,' he muttered.

'No. Tell us. Tell us all,' the voice insisted, as the speaker stepped forward into the light.

'Elisha!' Gehazi gasped. And all the others gasped with him.

'Tell them, Gehazi. Tell them the truth, for once. Tell

them how I rejected Naaman's reward, because the health and the peace that the man's cure brought was reward enough. Tell them how you sneaked off and pursued Naaman. Tell them how you lied to him and told him that I had changed my mind—that I wanted some of that reward to pass out among the other prophets. Then tell them how you took that money and those expensive clothes and hid them away for yourself! Tell them how you stole that reward, Gehazi—tell these men, these poor men, whose meal you have stolen, as well.'

'But what about his leprosy?' asked one of the men.

'His leprosy is his punishment,' Elisha sighed. 'But it was always my hope that it would also be his salvation—that his disfigured body would help him to see how disfigured his heart had become. That's why I came here tonight. To search him out. To see if he had changed. But he is, sadly, just the same as he always was.

'Gehazi,' Elisha sighed again. 'My servant, Gehazi. No one has ever done a better job of living up to his name. Denier. Diminisher. Belittler. You have seen God's power and watched his love at work, yet all you can do is resent it and tear it down and explain it away.

'I had nothing to do with that boy's birth. He was a gift from God. And it was God who brought him back to life when he died. God healed Naaman, as well, and I am confident that he can heal other lepers, too. All of you, in fact...' and here he looked at Gehazi, 'if you will only turn to him and trust him.'

The others jumped up, eagerly begging to be the first. But Gehazi said nothing. He gave Elisha one last, long bitter look. And then he limped off into the darkness, alone.

The Runaway's Tale

● ● ● ● ● ● ● ● ● ● ● ● ● ●

THE STORY OF JONAH

There's nothing nice about the story of Jonah. I know that many people think there is—that the Big Fish makes it the perfect story for little kids. But there's much more to the story than that.

You see, it's not about disobedience, even though the prophet Jonah did disobey God when he ran away. And it's not about being rescued, either, even though Jonah is saved from the fish and the city of Nineveh escapes destruction. No, the story of Jonah is all about prejudice. That's right—good old-fashioned racism and hate. And as far as I can tell, there's nothing nice about that.

Jonah admits as much. The people of Nineveh are not like him. And he refuses to go and speak to them, not because he is afraid of what they will do to him, but because he is

afraid *of what God will do for them, if they respond to his message.*

And that is why the story of Jonah ends so abruptly—not with an answer, but with a question: will Jonah lay aside his prejudices and choose to love whoever God loves? And, more importantly, will those who read his story do the same?

It didn't make any sense.

The words came to him in an instant, unexpected, as they always did. The voice was the same, unmistakable—it was God himself, the Maker of heaven and earth. But the message made no sense. No sense at all.

'Go to Nineveh, that great city, and speak my words to its people. For I have seen its wickedness.'

Jonah understood the part about wickedness. For Nineveh was the capital of Assyria. And Assyria was Israel's greatest enemy—not only because of her powerful army, which might sweep down at any time and destroy his people, but also because of her great immorality. Idol-worshippers. Pig-eaters. That's what the Assyrians were. Everything they did, and everything they believed was directly opposed to the holy Law that God had given Israel —the Law that Jonah had been taught to cherish and obey. They were Israel's arch enemies. Pagans, intent on destroying God's chosen people, the Hebrews. And yet, God had told Jonah to go and speak to them.

And that is what Jonah did not understand. That is what made no sense. For Jonah knew his prophet's job well: Speak God's word. Deliver God's message. And hope that those who received the message would listen and repent, and be granted God's mercy and blessing.

God's blessing on Nineveh? God's mercy—showered on

the enemy of God's people? Even the possibility was unthinkable. And that is why Jonah ran away.

It didn't make any sense. Not really. Jonah couldn't run away from God, and he knew it. But he didn't want any part of the mission that God had set for him, either. So he decided that the simplest solution would be for him to get as far away from Nineveh as possible. Nineveh was east; so Jonah headed west.

He went to Joppa, first—on the coast. And there he booked a passage on a ship set for Tarshish, at the western end of the Great Sea.

All went well, until a storm came thundering out of nowhere.

'This doesn't make any sense!' the captain thought. Every sailor was kneeling in prayer. But the passenger was down in the hold, fast asleep, as if nothing in the world was wrong.

'Wake up!' the captain shouted, shaking Jonah until he stirred. 'What's the matter with you? The ship is about to break in two and you are down here sleeping. Get up! Pray to your god! And maybe he will save us.'

Jonah prayed. Or, at least he bowed his head. But the storm did not subside. Not even a little. So the sailors drew straws, determined to find out who was responsible for their troubles. And the short straw went to Jonah.

'Who are you? Where do you come from?' they demanded. 'And what have you done that could have brought such evil upon us?'

Jonah looked at the sailors and sighed. There wasn't an Israelite among them. They were pagans, one and all. Pig-eaters. Idol-worshippers. How could they possibly understand?

'I am a Hebrew,' he explained. 'And I worship the Lord

God, the God who made the earth and sea—and everything else that is! He is the One I am running from. He is the One who is responsible for this storm.'

The sailors trembled. 'What can we do, then? Tell us— how do we appease your god? How do we stop the storm?'

'There is only one way,' said Jonah slowly. 'You must throw me into the sea.'

It didn't make any sense. The sailors should have jumped at Jonah's offer. They should have thrown him overboard and gone safely on their way. But they didn't. Instead, they took up their oars and rowed even harder for shore, hoping to outrun the storm.

'Is it possible?' Jonah wondered. 'Are these pig-eaters, these idol-worshippers, actually trying to save me?'

Whatever the intention, their efforts proved futile. For the harder they rowed, the higher the sea rose around them. Until, at last, there was no way out. Either Jonah would drown, or they *all* would!

So they fell to their knees again—and Jonah could hardly believe this—they prayed not to their own gods, but to the Lord!

'God! God of heaven and earth,' they cried, 'forgive us for what we are about to do.'

Then they tossed Jonah overboard, and immediately the sea grew calm. And as the prophet sank deeper and deeper beneath the waves, they worshipped the prophet's God and offered a sacrifice to his name.

It didn't make any sense. Somehow, Jonah was still alive! He could hear himself breathing. He could feel his heart beating. And the smell—phew!—he had never smelt anything so awful in his life! But when he opened his eyes, everything was dark.

He shook his head and tried to remember. He

remembered the crashing waves. He remembered struggling for the surface and saving each tiny bit of breath. And then, just before he passed out… he remembered! The fish! The biggest fish he had ever seen! And it was swimming straight for him.

'Is it possible?' Jonah wondered. 'It must be. It has to be! I am sitting in the belly of that fish!'

And, no, it still didn't make any sense. Jonah had disobeyed God. He knew he deserved to die. And yet God had preserved him and sent this fish—he was sure of it! And that meant, surely it meant, that God still had work for him to do, and that he would see the light of day, once more!

And so Jonah prayed a prayer. Not a prayer for help, but a prayer of thanksgiving, as if the help had already come. As if the belly of this fish were a temple, and he was seated in the midst of it—ribs standing tall like pillars, the odour of entrails rising like incense to Jonah's God.

'I was in danger. So I cried to God.
I cried to him and he answered me.
From the belly of hell I cried
And the Lord God heard my voice!

It was he who cast me in the sea,
Far beneath the crashing waves,
With the waters roaring round me,
And the surface like the sky.

And so I thought
That I had been banished,
Cut off from God
And his temple for ever.

'Down I went,
Down deeper and deeper,
Down to the feet of the mountains,
Seaweed wrapped around my head.

Down, still further down,
Down, and no escape.
And that is when you reached me
And rescued me from the watery pit.

Idol-worshippers don't understand.
Their requests count for nothing.
But I will give you thanks,
Offer sacrifices in your name,
For you are my great deliverer!'

Three days and three nights. That's how long Jonah waited in the belly of the fish. Then it belched him up onto dry land, and those words came pouring into his head again: 'Go to Nineveh, that great city, and tell them that I have seen their wickedness.'

It still didn't make any sense. Not to Jonah. But he wasn't about to argue, this time. So he travelled east, all the way to Nineveh. And when he got there, his mission made less sense than ever!

'This city is enormous!' sighed Jonah. 'It will take me days just to walk across it. How can my message possibly make any difference?'

But Jonah was determined not to end up in another fish's belly. So he started to preach.

'Forty days!' he said to anyone who would listen. 'Forty days to change your ways. Or else God is going to destroy your city.'

'This is useless!' Jonah sighed. 'These pig-eaters, these idol-worshippers, are never going to change.'

However, day after day, he preached. And day by day, the people of Nineveh began to take notice. There were just a few, at first, but soon the whole city was on its knees—from the humblest servant to the king himself—weeping and praying and asking God's forgiveness.

'This doesn't make any sense!' Jonah grumbled.

'No sense at all!' Jonah groused. 'You had the perfect opportunity, God, to destroy your enemy, and the enemy of your people. But you let it pass, and now—look at them— pig-eaters and idol-worshippers, praying, confessing, repenting and asking for forgiveness!

'Can you see, now, why I ran away? This won't last. They'll be up to their old tricks again in no time—you'll see! And then they'll be out to destroy us all over again.'

And at that moment, Jonah had an idea.

'I'll get out of the city,' he thought. 'I'll get out of the city and sit on the hillside and watch. Watch and wait for them to turn from God again. And then, maybe then—God will destroy the Ninevites once and for all!'

But his thoughts were interrupted by a voice.

'Jonah,' God called.

'Jonah!' God summoned. 'Do you really think it's right for you to be angry with me?'

But Jonah paid God no attention. He was too busy building a little shelter and stocking it with provisions, so that he could sit and watch the city's ruin.

So God got Jonah's attention another way. He made a tree grow up over Jonah's shelter, to shade him in the heat of the day. But just as Jonah had started to appreciate the shade, God sent a worm in the night to kill the little tree.

'This doesn't make any sense!' Jonah moaned. 'This tree was here one day, and gone the next. Now I'll have to sit and sweat.

'Life is so unfair!' he complained. 'I wish I was dead!'

And that's when the voice, the unmistakable voice, the voice of God himself, came pouring, once again, into Jonah's head.

'I'll tell you what makes no sense, Jonah,' the voice began. 'You grieve at the death of this tree, but you have no concern whatsoever for the people—the thousands of people—who live in the city below.

'Yes, they are idol-worshippers, as far from understanding me as a young child is from knowing its right or left hand. But I love them. And I have forgiven them. And if my ways are ever going to make any sense to you, Jonah, then you will have to lay aside your prejudices and learn to love them, too.'

The Heartless King's Tale

THE STORY OF HEROD

W hat do you think of when someone says 'Christmas'?
Stars and angels, right? Giving and peace and goodwill!
The story of the first Christmas is filled with those
images. But, like most stories, it has a villain, too. A selfish
and cruel villain who does everything he can to rob the story
of its wonder. A villain with a dark story all of his own.

I thought it would be interesting to set the story of
Christmas and Herod's story side by side—the story of Herod
and that of the child he tried to kill. Not only because the
stories are so different, but also because the difference offers
a vivid illustration of the contrast between good and evil—
between God's gift of life and one man's deadly ambition.

The night was crisp and clear. The stars shone bright like
candles. A mother cradled a child in her arms. And when

she closed her eyes and listened, she could almost hear the angels sing.

The old man in the palace, however, wasn't interested in angels. Ghosts were his companions. And they followed him, now, wherever he went.

It hadn't always been this way. When he was young, there was just too much to do. A kingdom to win. Power to establish. And enemies, more than he could count, to be dealt with and disposed of. And even when the bodies piled up—like stones stacked for his brand new temple—the ghosts stayed respectfully still.

How could he have known that they were just waiting—waiting for him to grow old and sick, waiting for him to grow tired, waiting for long and lonely winter nights.

The ghost of his uncle.

The ghost of his aunt.

The ghost of his wife.

The ghosts of his ambitious sons.

Murdered, each and every one. Murdered at his command. Murdered because they tried to take his throne.

'I am the King of the Jews!' he growled. Growled at the darkness. Growled at the walls. Growled at the noisy company of ghosts.

'I am the King of the Jews!' he growled again. 'Herod. Herod the Great!'

The walls did not answer. The darkness stayed silent and deep. But a knock at the door startled the king and sent him shaking.

'Who is it?' he whispered. 'What is it?' he called. And his heart slowed to a steady beat only when a servant stuck his head into the room.

'Visitors, Your Majesty,' the servant answered.

'At this hour?' the king shouted. 'Tell them to go away!'

'But they say it is urgent, Your Majesty. They have travelled, day and night, all the way from Babylon, following a star! A star which, they say, will lead them to our newborn king.'

Herod's heart started racing again. First the ghosts, and now this. Would he never be able to rest? And so, wearily he sighed, 'Send them in!'

The night was still and peaceful. The angels kept their silent watch. The carpenter kissed the baby and told his wife how he loved her.

But in the palace of the king, everyone was stirring.

'So you're looking for a king?' Herod asked his visitors.

'Yes,' one of them answered. 'The newborn King of the Jews.'

Herod wanted to say it. He really wanted to tell them, 'I am the King of the Jews!' But he had to control himself, he knew it, if he was to discover what these foreigners were up to.

'We have followed a star,' explained another visitor, 'all the way from Babylon. It led us here, to Judaea, and we thought you, of all people, might be able to tell us exactly where to find this new king.'

'And *why* would you want to find him?' asked Herod suspiciously.

'Why, so we could honour him with the gifts we have brought,' the visitor answered.

'So could you tell us, please?' added a third visitor. 'Even a hint would help—a prophecy, perhaps, from one of your holy books.'

'Stars and prophecies,' thought Herod. 'Stars and prophecies and ghosts. Why won't they leave me alone?' And for an instant, he considered sending these star-gazers away. But, what if... ? What if there really was a king, a baby king, out there? A king who would one day wrest the throne from him. Then he needed to know about it. He needed to find it. And he needed, most of all, to destroy it—before it had the chance to destroy him!

And so Herod shouted, 'Fetch the priests! No, the CHIEF priests! And the scribes, as well. Fetch anyone who can help us find this king!'

The night was a dark blue blanket. It lay over the hills and the shepherds and their sheep. And over the carpenter and his family, as they prepared at last to go to sleep.

But in the palace of the king, everyone was awake. Wide awake!

Herod snapped his fingers. 'Hurry!' he commanded. 'You are the experts in these things, so tell me: where do the prophets say the King of the Jews will be born?'

'Well, if it's the Messiah you mean,' answered one of the priests, 'then the prophets are very clear.'

'Bethlehem,' replied another priest, 'according to the words of the prophet Micah.'

'Excellent!' Herod smiled. 'Now you may go.'

'But if I may,' asked one of the chief priests, 'why is Your Majesty suddenly interested in this?'

'I have my reasons,' growled the king. 'Now, as I said, you may go.' And the priests hurried off into the night.

As soon as the priests had gone, Herod sent for the visitors. 'Tell me again,' he said. 'You have been following this star for how long?'

'Two years, Your Majesty,' answered one of the visitors.

Herod nodded his head. 'And so that would make this new king how old?'

'No more than two years,' the visitors explained.

'I see,' Herod nodded again. 'Well I have good news for you. My priests tell me that Bethlehem is the town you're looking for. It's not far from here.' And then, trying hard to look as innocent as possible, he added, 'Perhaps you could do me a favour? I, too, would like to honour this new king. So when you have found him, could you come and tell me exactly where he is?'

The night was bright with stars. But one star shone brightest of all. It hovered above the house of the carpenter and his family. It waited for the star-gazers, just as it had shown them the way. And then it watched as they knocked on the door, and were greeted by the sleepy carpenter, and went in to worship the child. And when they had offered their gifts and walked out of the house again, it winked goodbye and joined its brothers in the sky.

In Herod's palace, however, the king sat alone. Alone with his suspicions and fears. Alone with the ghosts.

'Yes, yes,' he muttered. 'I know what you're thinking. To make a ghost of a child is the greatest evil of all. But I can't take the chance, don't you see? No, I'm not worried about him growing up and taking my place. I'll have joined your company by then. What worries me is what might happen here and now. What if he has some legitimate claim to the throne? Or what if—God forbid!—he really is the Messiah? All my enemies would need to do is get hold of that child and use him against me. Moan all you want. Rustle the tapestries. Wail through the walls. Do what you will to frighten me. But I will not be moved from my course. When the star-gazers return, the child will die. And then he will be yours to deal with.'

The night crept over the star-gazers and swallowed them in sleep. They dreamed of shiny things—of stars and gold and bright perfume bottles. And then, something brighter still invaded their dreams—something shinier than their guiding star, purer than their golden gifts, and sweeter-smelling than all their balms and ointments. And they knew it could only be a messenger from God.

'Do not return to Herod,' the messenger warned them. 'For he is a wicked man, and he means to kill the boy. Sneak out of this country. Take another route home. And take the secret of the child with you.'

The star-gazers left at once. But Herod awoke with a start—roused by darker spirits, perhaps—and called for his guard.

'There is something wrong,' he said. 'Go to Bethlehem immediately, and bring me the visitors from the east.'

When the soldiers returned with news that the visitors had gone, Herod was not surprised. And he was not worried, either. For he had already devised a cruel alternative. So cruel that the soldiers, themselves, could hardly keep from weeping.

'You will kill every boy in Bethlehem!' he ordered. 'Every boy two years old or younger. You will be quick. You will be thorough. And you will show no mercy. This child will not escape me!'

As soon as the soldiers departed, the ghosts surrounded Herod. They clawed at his mind and tore at his heart. They raced around inside his head. And even as their numbers grew—child by murdered child—he would not be moved. Instead, he answered their dying screams with madman cries of his own: 'I am the King of the Jews! I am Herod the Great! And no one will take my throne from me!'

But as those cries echoed around his dark and ghostly bedchamber, the angels went to work again—warning the carpenter and his family and guarding them as they crept off safely and escaped into the night.

The Greedy Taxman's Tale

● ● ● ● ● ● ● ● ● ● ● ● ●

THE STORY OF ZACCHAEUS

N obody likes to pay taxes. But when the taxes go to an oppressive occupying government, and when the tax collector charges far more than he should just to line his own pocket, then it makes paying taxes that much harder to bear.

That's how it was, in Palestine, where Jesus lived. The Jewish people were ruled by the Romans, who had conquered them many years earlier. And their taxes enriched not only their conquerors, but also local tax collectors—fellow Jews who profited by collaborating with the Romans.

So tax collectors were the 'bad guys'. And you can understand why they were hated and despised and lumped, by

*polite society, with the lowest of the low. But Jesus didn't look
at it that way. He spent a lot of his time with folk who were
considered 'bad', and he received his share of criticism for that.
Yet he kept on doing it all the same, because he believed that no
one was out of reach of God's forgiveness and life-changing
love. Not even greedy tax collectors—like Zacchaeus.*

He loved the sound of coins.

The ringing and the jingling as they rained out of his
cupped hand.

The clicking and the clacking as they struck the wooden
table.

And the soft 'shoop-shoop' as he slid each one into its pile.

He loved the sound of coins. So there was no better time
than counting time. And his servants had strict instructions
that he was to be left alone, in peace and in quiet—
instructions that they were more than willing to keep, for he
was a hard and a miserable master, even at the best of times.

Drop a cup, or rattle a pot, or—heaven forbid!—break a
bowl or a pitcher, and an angry 'QUIET!' would echo from
the counting room. And so his servants tiptoed around the
house at this time of day, terrified of making even the
slightest noise.

Their fear and their anxiety meant nothing to him,
however. His servants were, after all, no more than coins as
far as he was concerned.

Five coins for the cook.

Two for the maid.

And one for the boy who minded his donkey.

And names? What was the point of learning names?
They never stayed that long. And anyway, it was the coins,
the coins that counted.

The coins he took from the citizens of Jericho.

The coins he passed on to the Roman Government.

And, most important of all, the coins he kept for himself!

That was the sum total of the tax collector's life. As for multiplying friendships, well, that was simply not prudent. For friends would only use the relationship to wriggle out of their obligation. And adding acquaintances? That was no more likely. For what time was left when the collecting and the counting was done? And who would want to be seen with a Roman collaborator, anyway?

No. Taking away the hard-earned money of Jericho, and dividing the piles between himself and the Romans—that was what mattered. And the coins. The sound of counting coins.

But, one day, there came another sound. A sound he couldn't ignore. The sound of laughter and cheering and crowds. And the tax collector was quick to react.

'Quiet!' he shouted. But the sound did not go away.

'Quiet, I said!' he shouted more loudly. And still the sound would not cease.

'QUIET!' he shouted a third time, as loudly as he could, banging his fist on the table and sending a tingling quiver through the coins. 'QUIET! I NEED QUIET!'

At last, the door creaked open, and a frightened whisper crept into the counting room. 'We're very sorry, master, but there is nothing we can do about the noise. It's coming from the street.'

'Then clear the rabble away!' the taxman growled. 'I have work to do. I need quiet.'

'But sir,' the voice pleaded, 'it's not just a few people. Everyone is out there. Everyone in Jericho!'

'Another holiday, I suppose,' groaned the tax collector. Then he launched into a tirade that the servant had heard a hundred times before.

'These people—they complain about paying their taxes. "It's a day's wage!" they moan. "How will we feed our families?" But give them a holiday, and they'll gladly lose a day's wage—the hypocrites!'

'But it's not a holiday, sir,' the servant answered. 'It's Jesus. The teacher and miracle-worker. Jesus has come to town!'

The tax collector groaned again. If there was one thing he hated more than noise, it was religion. It wasn't just the long list of rules—the dos and don'ts that would put any self-respecting taxman out of business. No, it was the money.

A coin for the priest.

A coin for the temple.

A coin for the sacrifice.

A coin for the poor.

And soon there were no coins left!

Again, he just couldn't understand the hypocrisy. The people hated him for what he took, but they were glad to give up a tenth of what they earned—and more!—so that priests, who were already fatter than him, could grow fatter still.

'I have no time for religion!' the taxman shouted. 'I have work to do!'

'Ah, but Jesus is different,' said the servant, thinking fast and hoping to win a little favour. 'They say he's the friend of tax collectors!'

'The friend of tax collectors?' sneered the taxman. 'That'll be the day!' And he slammed the door shut, nearly smashing his servant's nose.

And yet... as he sat there and counted, the taxman's curiosity grew.

'A religious teacher *and* the friend of tax collectors?' he wondered. 'How exactly does that work?' And then the tax collector grinned. For the first time in a long time, a mischievous smile found its way onto his face.

'Blessed are the shaker-downers,' he chuckled. 'And the rougher-uppers, and the over-chargers, and the bottom-liners. Blessed are the tax collectors!' he cheered. And at that moment, he made up his mind. He would leave his counting for the moment. He would venture out into the street. He would go to see this Jesus!

Now don't be mistaken. This was not a rash decision. As with everything else in his life, he counted the cost carefully. If he was spotted, he would certainly be cursed or spat upon or possibly even attacked by some angry taxpayer he'd overcharged or by some political fanatic who resented his connections with the Roman overlords. But a quick peep out of the window assured him that everyone's attention was turned to the street. So who would notice if someone—particularly someone small of stature like himself—were to sneak quietly behind the crowd and have a look?

And that's just what the tax collector did. He locked up his coins and he crept out the door and he picked his way carefully along the back of the crowd. But it wasn't long before he realized that there was one part of the equation he had not taken into account: Smallness was good for sneaking. Smallness was good for creeping. Smallness was especially good for not being seen. But as far as *seeing* was concerned, smallness was no good at all!

Yes, he could have wriggled and squirmed his way through the crowd. But that would have been unwise. For there, in that gap, was the broad backside of Benjamin the butcher, who had threatened him with a very sharp knife last time the taxes were due. And in the next gap were the unmistakably flat feet of shepherd Baruch—feet that had found their way to the tax collector's bottom a time or two. And over there? Well, what did it matter? The crowd was packed with people he had deceived or cheated or overcharged.

And then he saw it, standing tall at the end of the street. A single sycamore tree, with branches broad enough and full enough to conceal a small and nervous tax collector. And just high enough to give him a perfect view.

So over he crept and up he climbed, and because the crowd was so keen to see Jesus, no one noticed him. No one at all.

The tax collector, however, could see everything. There was Jesus, or at least that's who he assumed it was, greeting the cheering crowd. And there were the town dignitaries, of course, the rich and respected ones, pushing their way to the front. He knew what they were saying, even though he was too far away to hear:

'Come to *my* house, Jesus!'

'Eat at *my* table, Jesus!'

'Visit *my* home, Jesus!'

There was nothing hospitable about this, of course. Each and every one of those hypocrites was just anxious to hear the 'Ooohs' and 'Aaahs' of the crowd when this famous holy man agreed to honour their house with his presence.

But as the tax collector watched, the most remarkable thing began to happen. With every greeting, with every request, Jesus gently shook his head—'No thank you.'

'Is he leaving town so quickly?' the tax collector wondered. 'Or has he already made some other arrangements? If not, he had better make up his mind soon, for he's almost at the end of the street.'

And, at that very moment, Jesus stopped. And looked up. And spoke one word and one word only.

'Zacchaeus.'

The tax collector hardly knew what to do. He thought

he was hidden. He thought he was safe. And besides, it had been so long since he'd heard his name spoken, it hardly seemed as if it belonged to him at all. The servants called him 'sir', and the townspeople had their own selection of names. And as for anybody else. Well, there wasn't anybody else. Not until now, anyway.

'Zacchaeus!' Jesus called again. 'Zacchaeus, come down!'

And with that the crowd began to mock and to point and to howl. 'The tax collector! Look! The tax collector is up in the tree!' But their laughter collapsed into stunned silence at Jesus' next words.

'Zacchaeus,' he said again, 'I'm coming to *your* house, today.'

Leaves. Leaves against leaves—that was the only sound, as Zacchaeus climbed slowly down the tree. But with each branch, a new thought went racing through his head:

'Why is Jesus doing this?'

'Is this some kind of trick?'

'What will the people do?' and

'Is there anything in the pantry?'

It had been ages since anyone had visited his home, so Zacchaeus simply muttered, 'Come this way,' and hoped that he could remember what to do. As for the crowd, their surprise soon turned into something uglier.

'He's a thief! He's a cheat! He's a sinner!' the crowd complained. 'Why is Jesus eating with him?' Part of it was jealousy. And part of it was confusion. Holy men ate with good people—that's what they were used to. But this was different. And in that difference lay the explanation for what happened next.

Maybe it had to do with what Jesus said. Or maybe with what he did. Or maybe it was no more than Jesus' willingness to call Zacchaeus by name and offer to be his friend. But when dinner was over, Zacchaeus came out of his house again, not creeping, not sneaking, but standing tall (or at least as tall as he was able!).

'I have something to say to you,' he announced to the crowd. 'Something to say to you all. I'm sorry. I'm sorry for cheating you and deceiving you and making myself rich at your expense.' And then he waved his hand and his servants came out of the house as well, carrying bags of coins.

'My life was all about taking away. But from now on, that will be different. Half of all I own, I will give to the poor. And whatever I have stolen from anyone, I will multiply by four and return to them, here and now.'

Someone gasped. Someone shouted. And soon the whole crowd cheered.

'Salvation has come to this house!' cheered Jesus along with them. But as Zacchaeus tore open the moneybags and his fortune spilled out through his fingers, all he could hear were the coins, the sound of the coins, ringing and jingling, and somehow more beautiful than ever—now that he was giving them away!

The Politician's Tale

● ● ● ● ● ● ● ● ● ● ● ●

THE STORY OF PILATE

Sometimes, it's hard to know exactly what a biblical character was like. You piece together the information as best you can, but you're still not sure you've captured the person.

Take Pilate, for example—the Roman governor who presided over the trial and execution of Jesus. Some people have seen him as a basically good man who got caught in a difficult situation. Others have pictured him as weak and indecisive. Personally, I think the clue to his character lies in something he said to Jesus.

'I have come to tell the truth,' Jesus explained, during his trial. And all Pilate could say in return was, 'What is truth?'

You see, there are some people who try hard to live by what they believe is true. And there are others that fail to do *that. But the really scary people are the ones who don't believe that there is any truth, any right or wrong, at all. I think that's the kind of person Pilate was. And even though you may find him charming and amusing, his disregard for any truth beyond himself may well make him the baddest baddy of them all.*

Pilate rubbed his hands together and smiled at his new assistant. 'Well then, are we ready to get to work?'

Marcus smiled politely in return and nodded, 'Yes, Governor. And may I say what a pleasure it is to be working for someone who truly seems to enjoy his job.'

Pilate winked and gave the young man a knowing look. 'Excellent!' he grinned. 'Butter up the boss on your very first day. Someone's taught you well, my boy.'

'No, I meant it, sir,' Marcus responded. 'Some of my past employers just seemed to be putting in their time—waiting for that next holiday or the retirement villa by the sea.'

'Ah yes,' Pilate nodded. 'I know the type. I've worked for a few myself. But I can assure you that things are different here. I like what I do! It's difficult, sometimes. And it's always risky. But for my money, it's still the best game in town!'

'Game, sir?' asked Marcus.

'What else would you call it?' said Pilate, dropping down into his chair. 'Keep the peace. Keep the revenues rolling in. Keep Caesar happy. Those are the official rules.'

'And the object of the game, as well,' Marcus added.

Pilate chuckled. 'No, my boy. The object of the game is for "yours truly" to keep his job. And, with any luck, to keep climbing up that empire-sized ladder.'

Marcus looked a bit confused, now. 'But, sir? What

about duty? What about justice? What about right and wrong?'

Pilate's chuckle grew into a laugh. 'You do have a lot to learn, don't you?' Then he stood up on his chair and stuck his arms straight out from his sides. 'I've always thought it was a bit like walking on an aqueduct.'

'An aqueduct, sir?'

Pilate peered down at his assistant. 'You mean to tell me that you've never walked on an aqueduct? Why when I was a boy, growing up in the Roman countryside, there was nothing I enjoyed better. My friends and I would climb up on top of the tallest one we could find. The water would be rushing down the middle, faster than any river. But along the stonework at the edge, there was just enough room to walk.'

'But wasn't that dangerous, sir?'

'Of course it was dangerous! That was the point! Fall off one side and you'd smash your head on the ground below. Fall off the other side, and the water would carry you halfway to Sicily before they could fish you out. But if you held your arms out just right—leaning a little this way and a little that way and watching carefully for which way the wind was blowing—then you could do it, and not get killed.

'That's what it's like being the governor of Palestine. A little justice here. A little oppression there. A touch of mercy. A hint of brutality. It's all the same really—just so long as you keep your balance. Just so long as you don't fall off.'

'And you enjoy that, sir?'

'More than anything, my boy,' Pilate grinned. Then he hopped onto the floor and plopped back into his chair. 'Every day is different. Every day, an adventure. So let's see what today brings. Secretary!' he called. 'Send in the first appointment.'

A short, round, bald-headed man stuck his head into the room.

'I'm terribly sorry, Governor,' he apologized, 'but I'm afraid you're going to have to come into the courtyard for this one. It's another one of their holy days, and they say they'll be defiled if they come into the building.'

'Yes, yes,' Pilate sighed. 'I know the drill.'

But the look on Marcus' face suggested that he did not. 'Defiled, sir?' he asked.

'It's a religious thing,' Pilate explained. 'The Jews are obsessed with this notion that they are God's special people. Which, of course, makes the rest of us somewhat less-than-special. So they are forbidden to have any close contact with us—to come into our homes, for example—in case it makes them unfit to participate in their religious rituals. That's the gist, anyway.'

'So what do we do?' Marcus asked.

'We humour them,' Pilate answered, sticking out his arms again and tippy-toeing forward. 'It's all about balance, remember? Our little walk into the courtyard will make the Jewish leaders happy. And, I don't know about you, but I could use the exercise!' And then Pilate chuckled. 'As they say, when in Jerusalem…'

'But what do you think they want, sir?' Marcus asked.

'Publius?' Pilate inquired, turning to his secretary.

And the secretary just rolled his eyes. 'It's another Messiah, Governor.'

Pilate clapped his hands together happily. 'Excellent! Did you hear that, Marcus? Another Messiah! We should be finished by lunch!'

'A Messiah, sir?' Marcus asked. 'I'm afraid…'

'Yes, of course. You're new.' And then Pilate stopped for a moment. 'The Messiah is a Jewish legend. The Christ. The

Anointed One. The King of the Jews. It's all the same, and it all has to do with their belief that, one day, their god will send a powerful leader to set them free from their enemies.'

'Their enemies?' asked Marcus. 'And that would be... ?'

'Us! Yes, that's right,' Pilate grinned. 'And I take it as a sign of our efficiency as conquers and overlords that so many of these Messiahs have been popping up recently. I suppose we've dealt with—what?—one a month?'

'At least, sir,' moaned Publius. 'A nuisance, if you ask me, sir.'

'Yes, well, you have to deal with the paperwork, don't you? I, on the other hand, only have to deal with the Messiahs. And frankly, I find them quite fun!'

'Fun, sir?' asked Publius and Marcus, together.

'Of course! Messiahs come in two basic shapes, you see. The hairy, under-nourished, wide-eyed, fanatically-religious shape. And the don't-turn-your-back-on-me-or-I'll-stick-a-knife-in-your-neck political revolutionary shape.

'Now the first kind is no trouble at all. You listen to them rant and rave for a few minutes, and then send them off to be flogged.

'As for your revolutionary types... well, it's the rules of the game, isn't it? Young Marcus...'

Marcus thought hard. 'Umm... Keep the peace. Keep the revenues rolling in... Keep Caesar happy!'

'Excellent! And because your basic revolutionary Messiah is all for starting trouble and disrupting trade and booting poor Caesar out of the country, what do you do? You crucify him. Simple as that!

'And so,' Pilate concluded, grinning that grin and rubbing his hands together again, 'let's see what kind of Messiah we have today!'

As Pilate entered the courtyard, he glanced at the

prisoner. The man stood quiet and still. His hair was matted, his eyes tired. It looked as if someone had beaten him up.

Next, he glanced at the crowd, then turned to his assistant and whispered, 'All the big shots are here—the Jewish leaders and their council. I'm guessing that we've got your basic religious type Messiah to deal with.'

Finally, he turned to the crowd itself. 'So tell me. What is this man charged with?'

The accusations shot forth, more fiercely than Pilate had ever heard them before.

'He stirs up the nation!'

'He tells us not to pay our taxes!'

'He says he is Christ—the King!'

'It seems like he's broken all the rules of the game,' observed Marcus.

Pilate just nodded. 'So you want me to put him to death? Is that it?' Pilate said to the crowd. 'Well, let me talk with him, first. It's Roman law that needs to be satisfied here.'

'And it will keep them in their place!' he whispered to Marcus.

Pilate took the prisoner aside and looked him straight in his swollen and bloodshot eyes.

'So you're the King of the Jews then, are you?'

'That's what they say,' shrugged the prisoner.

'Look,' Pilate answered, 'I don't care what *they* say. What I need to know is what *you* say. Are you the King of the Jews or not?'

The prisoner sighed, as if he were tired—not from lack of sleep, but for lack of being understood.

'I have a kingdom, yes. But it's not the kind of kingdom you're thinking of. If it were, my followers would be here, fighting for me.'

Now it was Pilate's turn to sigh. 'So let me get this straight,' he continued. 'You say you *are* a king, then?'

'*You* say that I am a king. But I was sent into this world for a different reason. I was sent to speak the *truth*.'

'Truth?' chuckled Pilate. 'TRUTH? What is truth?' Then he shook his head and walked back to his aide.

'Well?' asked Marcus.

'Well, he's not political—that's for sure. And he doesn't strike me as your typical fanatic, either. He's different, I'll grant you that. But he doesn't deserve to die.'

And that's what Pilate told the crowd: 'I find no crime, here. No crime at all.'

But if Pilate thought that would satisfy them, then he was wrong. They started shouting again—louder even than the first time.

'But he's stirring up the people! It started up in Galilee, and now it's spread all the way down here to Judaea.'

'They obviously hate this man,' Pilate whispered to Marcus. 'And they're not going to go away until I do something...' And then Pilate grinned and snapped his fingers.

'Did you say he's from Galilee?' Pilate shouted to the crowd. 'Well, that's not under my control. Herod Antipas is in charge of Galilee, and as it happens, he's here, in town, for your Passover festival. Why don't you take the prisoner to Herod and let him decide what to do?'

The crowd grunted and moaned. But they were eager to have their way, so they grabbed the prisoner and dragged him off to see Herod.

'There's another lesson for you,' Pilate beamed. 'When you're having trouble making a decision—or when a decision is likely to make trouble for you—pass the responsibility on to someone else!'

Pilate escorted Marcus back into his office, but it wasn't long before Publius stuck his head into the room again.

'It's that Messiah, Governor. I'm afraid he's back.'

'But what about Herod?' Pilate asked.

'It seems he's learned that lesson about passing on difficult cases, too.'

'Then he's a smarter man than I've given him credit for,' Pilate noted. 'I'll have to invite him over sometime.' Then he marched out into the courtyard, looking as 'official' as possible.

'I have already made my decision,' he announced to the crowd. 'This man has committed no crime!'

But the crowd would not be pacified, and they shouted even more loudly.

'All right! All right!' Pilate announced, 'How about this? Every year, during your festival, I release a prisoner, as a gesture of goodwill towards the community. Why don't I let this man go?'

'No!' shouted one of the priests. 'Free Barabbas, instead!'

'Barabbas?' asked Marcus.

'A thief and a murderer,' explained Pilate. 'And also something of a local hero.'

And that is why the crowd began to chant, 'We want Barabbas! We want Barabbas! We want Barabbas!'

'Ah well,' sighed Pilate, 'I hate to do it, but it's the rules of the game... All right, then,' he announced to the crowd. 'I shall set Barabbas free!' And then he pointed to the prisoner, 'But what shall I do with this man?'

'Crucify him!' the crowd chanted. 'Crucify him!'

'But he's done nothing wrong!' Pilate called back.

'He's made himself a king!' someone shouted. 'And that makes him an enemy of the true king—Caesar!'

'Yes!' shouted someone else, 'So if you set him free, then that makes you Caesar's enemy, too!'

'The hypocrites!' Pilate muttered to Marcus. 'They hate Caesar, maybe even more than they hate this man. But it's obvious. They're willing to say anything that will get him crucified. And frankly, I can't afford to let this crowd get any further out of hand. And so I suppose that it comes down to the rules of the game, once again.'

'Even if you have to execute an innocent man?' asked Marcus.

Pilate smiled. 'Well, I've thought of a way round that, as well. Publius, fill me a basin of water. And bring me a clean towel.'

'Do you see this?' called Pilate to the crowd. 'I am innocent of this man's blood!' Then he plunged his hands into the water, and ordered his soldiers to beat the prisoner and take him off to be crucified.

'Nice touch, don't you think?' remarked Pilate, once the crowd had gone. 'If I've made the right decision, then I'm the hero. And if I've made the wrong one, well, I think I'm covered there, as well.'

Marcus was not convinced. 'But don't you worry that it makes you seem weak and indecisive?'

'Not if I keep my balance!' smiled Pilate, sticking out his arms again. 'Now let's get back to work.'

The rest of the day was uneventful.

Some of the Jewish leaders complained about the sign that had been nailed on the prisoner's cross. Someone else came by to claim the man's body once he'd died. And, somewhere in the middle of the afternoon, the weather suddenly turned worse than anyone could remember.

'Well, what do you say, Marcus?' asked Pilate, as they

prepared, at last, to go home. 'A good day's work?'

'I suppose so, sir,' Marcus answered. 'But I can't help feeling just a little uncomfortable. I mean, we released a murderer, and executed what looked like an innocent man.'

'Yes, that's true,' Pilate said. 'But did we win the game? That's the important question. And if you look at it that way, we did extraordinarily well. We kept the peace. We prevented a riot...'

'And the dead man, sir?'

'Ah, yes,' mused Pilate. 'The dead man. Well, I don't think we'll be hearing from him again. Do you?'

The Robber's Tale

Some people say that your whole life flashes before your eyes just before you die. I don't know if that's true or not, because I've never faced that situation! But what if it were true? And what if you had the chance to write it down, or tell it to someone? Then it might sound something like the story you are about to read.

It wasn't my fault. Not really. My brother was older than me. And, you know how it is. You look up to your brother, especially when you're little. And you want to do what he does...

Well, my brother was a thief. And even though he was only eleven or twelve when he started, he got good fast. He had this innocent face, for a start—round chubby cheeks that old ladies just loved to pinch. So they trusted him.

He was quick, too. He could snatch a coin off a table so

fast that it looked like his hand had never moved at all!

And best of all, he could talk. Boy, could he talk! One story after another—lie after lie after lie. And all the time with that smile on his face. My brother could talk his way out of anything!

Once—and I had nothing to do with this, I swear!—he stole this chicken from old Simeon's wife. And not just any chicken, of course. But her favourite chicken. The one with the big brown spot on its back! So, there he was, running down the street, with this chicken tucked under his arm, when who should come bustling out of a door in front of us but the old lady herself!'

Now, Simeon's wife was the chief cheek pincher in our village. So when she saw my big brother, right there in front of her, she threw wide her huge arms, and like some enormous lobster, began to flex those fat pinching fingers. Escape? Escape was out of the question, for Simeon's wife was also the widest woman in town. We tried to avoid her. We really did. But our speed and her bulk resulted in one huge collision—and my brother and I found ourselves sitting, dazed, on our backsides before her!

'Now where are you boys off to in such a hurry?' she grinned, pinching his cheeks (and then mine, for good measure). But before either of us could say a thing, she spotted her spotty hen.

The big woman's smile turned down into a frown. But before it could fall into a full-fledged scowl, my brother blurted out, 'We were bringing your chicken back to you. That's why we were in such a hurry! We found it in... Anna's yard. That's right! And we thought maybe it had wandered there or—God forbid!—that old Anna had stolen your chicken. Anyway, we watched her, and when she went into her house, we grabbed it as fast as we could and ran and… Here—it's all yours again!'

Simeon's wife just looked at my brother, and then, slowly, her frown turned into a puzzled stare.

'But, Anna?' she pondered, 'Why would Anna want to take my chicken?'

'Jealousy!' my brother jumped back in, eager to save his story. 'That has to be it. After all, it's not everyone who has a chicken that looks like that!'

'That's true,' the old woman nodded. And then she leaned nearer and whispered, 'And I'm sure you're too young to know this, but they say that Anna has always fancied my Simeon—the most handsome man in the village, if I say so myself!'

So she bought the story. And instead of smacking us round the head or dragging us off to the local judge, she pinched our cheeks one more time and rewarded us each with a shiny silver coin!

My brother grinned and strutted as we made our way back home. But I was still a little worried.

'What if she talks to Anna?' I said.

'Oh, I don't think that's going to happen,' he chuckled, as he pulled a piece of woven cloth out from under his shirt. 'I grabbed this out of the old lady's basket,' he laughed. 'Between all the pinching and hugging. It's her own special pattern, and when it gets dark, I know just what we're going to do with it!'

'But it's the Sabbath!' I said.

'That's right!' he grinned again. 'Everybody will be at home, praying and reading and stuff. Everybody but you and me!'

And so, later that night, we crept out of our house and across the village and into Anna's yard. And while I watched, my brother quietly wrung the neck of every chicken in her yard (did I mention that he could be vicious, as well?), and left that piece of cloth behind as 'evidence'.

There was a lot of commotion in the village, the next morning—questions and rumours and accusations. And I understand that the two women never talked to one another again.

As for my brother, he just got better and better at his chosen profession. Pickpocketing, sheep-stealing, breaking and entering—there wasn't anything he couldn't do. And soon, we'd built up a little gang. (Well, he did actually, because, as I've said, I never did any of the *real* stealing. I was a lookout, mostly. Just along for the ride.)

We started moving from place to place. We hit the villages first because they were the easiest. But as folk started to recognize us, we had to aim for the larger towns, and then the cities. Get lost in the crowds—you know what I mean.

Crowds can be a great cover, actually. That's what my brother always said. All those people, bunched together—jostling, bumping, pushing. And if a hand should slip into a pocket, a pouch, or a purse, who would notice? Markets are good, public executions aren't bad, but nothing beats a good old-fashioned religious festival! Nobody's on their guard, you see. They're all feeling good and holy, and they walk around with the mistaken notion that everyone else is feeling good and holy, too!

There was this time, for example, up in Galilee—near the sea—when all these people were listening to this teacher. His name was Jesus and he was another one of those Messiah wannabes. You know—'Follow me and I will lead you to God.' That sort of thing. Anyway, we were doing pretty well. The crowd couldn't keep its eyes off him, which meant, of course, that they weren't paying attention to us at all!

He was telling this story, about a guy who gets fed up with his dad, runs off with his inheritance, and gambles it all away—or something like that. When the money's all gone, this guy drags himself back home again. You know what the father's going to do—smack him round the head (like Simeon's wife should have done to us!). But no! The father rewards him—gives him rings and robes and a fancy feast! I have to admit it was the most unlikely story I had ever heard. So I glanced over at my brother, to get his reaction. And he was fuming!

I thought, for a moment, that he was angry with me—for listening to the story instead of, you know, attending to the 'business'. But it was the teacher—that's who had him so worked up.

'Now there's the thief!' he muttered. 'He doesn't work—I can promise you that. But somebody's feeding him and taking care of him. He fills their heads with lies, and they love him for it. Let's get out of here!'

And so, even though there were hundreds of purses left to pinch, we headed out across the hills and into the nearest town.

A couple of years went by—I was about eighteen or nineteen by then—and we started to get a little cocky. Success does that to you, and the problem is that you start to get sloppy, too. Soon you start to believe that you can pull off anything—even stealing from the Romans.

That was our big mistake. If we'd stuck to Jews and Samaritans and the odd caravan trader, we'd still be working today. But someone told my brother about all the treasure hidden away in this centurion's house, down in Jerusalem. So he planned it, he broke in, and he grabbed it.

(And as for his beating the centurion nearly to death, well I can't say, can I? I was outside. The lookout. Remember?) Anyway, what we didn't know was that the old boy was retiring, and that a bunch of soldiers had chosen that very night to surprise him with a party. So the surprise was on us and, surrounded, we surrendered. What else could we do?

My brother tried to talk his way out of it. But the Romans didn't really understand our language. So instead of a pinch on the cheek, all he got was a hard smack in the mouth. Then they dragged us off to jail.

When he came to, my brother just sat there, speechless, not for hours, but for days. I'd never seen him so quiet, but each time I tried to say something—you know, start up a conversation, lighten the mood—he growled at me. And, I got the message.

Finally, he spoke. But it wasn't what I expected him to say.

'Did you ever wish you could start all over again?'

I was a little confused. 'You mean, like planning the robbery better? Or staying away from the Romans?'

'No,' he sighed. 'I mean—life. Starting over again. Getting another chance. Like the story that teacher told, about the boy and his father. You remember?'

'But you thought that was stupid,' I reminded him.

'Yeah, well, I guess I never thought I'd need a second chance. I was always so good at talking my way out of things. But now, now that it's all over, I guess I feel different.'

'What do you mean, all over?' I asked. 'We're getting out of here, right?'

And that's when he gave me the 'look'. The big brother to little brother 'look'. The look that said he thought I was some kind of an idiot.

'You don't get it, do you?' he said. 'They're going to kill us. These are the Romans we're talking about. They're going to drag us out of here, hang us on a cross, and crucify us!'

'But why?' I asked. 'Why? I mean, I didn't do anything. I was just the lookout. You can tell them that, can't you?'

But my brother just sighed and shook his head and turned his face again, silent, to the wall.

He was right, of course. Not two days later, they woke us up, tied each of us to a cross, and before the sun came up, there we were, just hanging there, waiting to die.

I screamed for a little while. 'It's not my fault,' I pleaded. 'It's not fair!'

But the soldiers just laughed, and the growing crowd didn't want to know. So after a while, I shut up. It was hard to breathe, hanging like that, and harder still to talk. Maybe that's why my brother never said a word.

Time passed. I don't know how much. And then a whole parade of people came marching up the hill. There was wailing and weeping on one side and cheering on the other. And then they raised a third cross up between us.

I turned my head and looked at the guy. He was a mess! Cuts and bruises all over his body, and blood pouring down his face He must have done something awful, I thought. And as bad as I felt, I was glad I wasn't in his shoes.

And then I looked closer. And I couldn't believe what I saw.

It was Jesus! You know, the teacher we saw up in Galilee!

I tried to get my brother's attention. But, no, he wouldn't even look my way. So I thought, hey, why not try to win a little respect from him, cheer him up, maybe, right at the end. Show him that I'm not the idiot brother he always thought I was.

So I turned to this Jesus and I said, 'Hey! Hey! They say you're the Messiah, right? God's Special Guy. Well, if you're

such a big shot, why don't you do something about this? Why don't you snap your fingers or say the magic word and get us all out of this mess?'

It was good, I thought. Funny, you know. So I glanced at my brother, just to get his reaction. And I couldn't believe it—he was giving me that 'idiot' look again!

'What is wrong with you?' he sighed. 'We're all going to die here. Aren't you afraid of that? And aren't you even more afraid of God, and what he'll do to us? I mean, we're here because we deserve it. We've been thieves all our lives. But look at this man. Look at him! He's done nothing wrong. Not a thing.'

And then he turned to the teacher. And I don't know—maybe it was just sweat—but I'd swear there were tears in my brother's eyes. And that's when he said it.

'Jesus. Jesus, will you remember me when you come into your kingdom?'

And Jesus nodded. And Jesus forced a little smile. And Jesus said, 'Yes. Today, truly, you will be with me in paradise.'

Yeah, I know what you're thinking. I suppose I should have said something, too. But, hey, what for? It was my brother, my brother who was the bad guy. My brother who was the thief. I was just a lookout. Honest. I never did anything wrong, not really. Like I said at the beginning, it wasn't my fault...

The Coward's Tale

Sometimes the worst kind of badness is the badness inside you, the badness you can't seem to fix. You say something hurtful to somebody. Or you lose your temper. Or you lie about something. And a minute after you do it, you feel bad, and you wish you could take it all back. But you can't, because you're embarrassed or afraid or worried that something worse might happen if you try to put it right.

Everybody feels that way, sometimes. Peter did. He was one of Jesus' followers, one of his closest friends. But time and time again, he found himself doing and saying things that disappointed Jesus—things he was sorry for later. This story is about one of those times. And even though Peter tried, he still couldn't find a way to fix and forgive himself. He needed someone to do it for him. And fortunately, that someone was *there, hanging on a cross, rising from the dead, and waiting for him, on the beach.*

The fire was warm. And the end of his beard and the edge of his sandals were just about dry.

His belly was full. The taste of fish lingered in his mouth, and a crusty bit of bread clung to his moustache.

He'd just had a big catch. His friends sat round about him. He should have been happy. But he wasn't.

His best friend of all was there, you see. The one who had died and come back to life. The one he had abandoned and denied.

There had been a fire, then, as well. And a cold night. And a silent moon. And in the place of the comrades who now chattered around him, there sat strangers and enemies.

Peter remembered it well. Too well. It was a serving girl who had spoken first. She had been gazing through the flames for some time, trying to catch his eye and to get a good look at his face. But Peter had sat still, still as stone—hunched over, silent, afraid. It was her voice that had set him shivering.

'This man was with him, too!' she pointed. 'With Jesus, who they arrested!'

Peter held himself tight, to stop the shaking. He was afraid. He was afraid! The guards. The arrest. The torches. The fighting. His friends were scattered, his master in custody. He was afraid! Who wouldn't be? And surely that is why he had blurted out, almost without thinking, 'Woman! I do not know the man!'

It was a lie. Of course it was a lie! But if that busybody hadn't stuck her nose in...

Before he could fashion his excuse, however, another voice called out from the darkness. 'Yes, you're right. I've seen him with Jesus, too! You're one of his followers, aren't you?'

'No! No!' Peter shouted, wishing that somehow he could disappear, hoping to heaven that he could just wake up from this nightmare. 'No, I am not one of them!'

But the strangers would not be quiet. They would not give up. He was the focus of attention, now. And all eyes— he could feel them—were gazing, peering, inspecting and identifying, each and every one trained on him.

Jesus' career had been so public, the miracles so amazing, the crowds so huge. Thousands and thousands of people had seen Jesus and his friends together, with Peter the biggest and noisiest of the bunch. And so it was inevitable that another voice, a third voice, should come to the same conclusion as the rest.

'Yes!' someone called. 'Definitely! He's from Galilee. He's one of them!'

'No!' shouted Peter, his heart racing and his hands sweating.

'No!' he repeated, frantic and afraid. 'I NEVER EVEN KNEW THE MAN!'

And then the rooster crowed.

Jesus had said this would happen. In the midst of Peter's boasting about how he would fight to the death for his master, Jesus had contradicted him.

'No, Peter,' he had whispered. 'Before this night is through, before the cockerel calls to the coming dawn, you will deny that you ever knew me.'

Peter had wept bitterly that day, mixing his tears with the morning dew. And he could find no excuse—not fear, not panic, not fate—to chase away the guilt he felt at having turned his back on his friend.

A chunk of wet sand, caked to the side of his leg, dried through just enough to fall off. But it left behind a filmy, sandy residue that irritated him until he brushed it away. And Peter couldn't help thinking that it was just the same way with his guilt.

They'd met a few times—he and Jesus—since that night. That night before Jesus had died. But now, Jesus was alive again! And the shock and the joy of those meetings had shaken away great chunks of Peter's guilt and shame. But it wasn't all gone. And because Jesus hadn't mentioned his denial, Peter didn't want to bring it up.

And that's why this man with a full belly and warm feet and one amazing, resurrected friend wasn't very happy. There was something he needed to do. Something he couldn't bring himself to say.

There was another reason, too: fish.

When they'd first met—he and Jesus—Peter was a fisherman. But Jesus had promised to make him something else—a fisher of *men*. More than that, Jesus had called him a rock, and when Peter had found the confidence to stand up and say what all the disciples had been thinking—that Jesus was the Messiah—he had received the master's praise for his insight.

But where was Peter now? Sitting on the sand at the side of Lake Galilee. That's where he was. Back where he had started, doing his old job, fishing for fish. But what else was he fit for? What good was a rock that turned to sand at the first whiff of danger?

And how could he be a fisher of men when he couldn't even admit his friendship with Jesus to just three people? Perhaps being a fisher of fish was all he was good for, after all.

A gull cried. The fire popped. Then it belched out a puff

of smoke. Jesus watched the smoke melt into the air, then he turned to Peter and said, 'Simon, son of John, do you love me more than these?'

Surprised by both the suddenness of the question and by the question itself, Peter had to stop and think. 'Do I love him more than these? These what? These other disciples? Well, of course I do. Didn't I say once that even if all the others left him, I would remain?'

And then Peter hung his head in shame. 'But I didn't, did I?' he remembered again. 'I ran and hid like everybody else. And worse.'

Meanwhile, Jesus was poking holes in the sand, waiting for an answer. Peter knew what he wanted to say. But after what he'd done, would Jesus believe him, or just think him the worst kind of hypocrite? And so, with his eyes fixed on the sand, he said, both as quietly and a firmly as he could, 'Yes, Lord, you know that I love you.'

Jesus set the stick down and looked at Peter's face. 'Then feed my lambs,' he said.

This wasn't the response that Peter expected. He thought that Jesus was finally getting round to the 'denial' business. That he'd tell him off, call him a no-good liar or a coward or a phoney. Peter could understand that. It was the least he deserved.

Or maybe, on the other hand, Peter imagined, Jesus would turn to him and say, 'It's all right. I understand. Don't worry about it any more.'

But he didn't do either of those things. All he said was, 'Feed my lambs.'

And then it dawned on him. Perhaps, when Jesus had said, 'Do you love me more than these?' he hadn't meant 'these disciples' at all. Perhaps he'd meant 'these fish'. Well, not the fish themselves, but the fishing gear—the nets and tackle and rope. Maybe Jesus was saying, 'Do you really intend to go back to being a fisher of fish? Or do you want to carry on working for me?'

Peter was going to ask, but Jesus got there first. 'Simon, son of John,' he repeated, 'do you love me?'

There was that question again! Perhaps Jesus hadn't heard him the first time. The answer had been rather quiet. But Peter was feeling more confident now. So he looked at Jesus this time. Well, glanced at him, really. And he gave him the same answer. 'Yes, Lord, you know that I love you.'

'Then feed my sheep,' replied Jesus.

'That's it!' thought Peter. 'He does want me back! He still wants me to be a fisher of men. And he still believes I can be a rock. And now he wants me to be a shepherd, as well—to take care of his followers! He wants me back. He thinks I can do it. Everything is all right again!'

Peter leaped to his feet, ready to throw his nets on the fire, when Jesus took him by the arm, led him away from the others and asked him, one more time.

'Do you love me?'

'Well, this is silly!' thought Peter. 'We've dealt with that already. Surely, Jesus had heard him the first two times. What was the point of saying it... a third time?'

Peter shut his eyes and sighed. Some rock he was turning out to be. More like rocks-for-brains! Peter saw it all, now. Jesus was giving him his job back, yes. But he was giving him something more: A chance to make up for those other three times. A chance to say what he should have said that night. A chance to speak the truth from his heart. A chance to deal with it, once and for all.

Peter opened his eyes and wiped them dry with the back of his hand. Then he looked right at Jesus, right into his

eyes, and said, 'Lord, you know everything. You know that I love you.'

And in return, Jesus smiled a knowing, everything-will-be-all-right kind of smile, and said for the third time, 'Then feed my sheep.'

They wandered slowly back to the others. The fire was warm. Peter's belly was full. He was surrounded by his friends. And now, for the first time in a long time, Peter was happy. Not only because his best friend was alive again. But also because something had come back to life in him, as well.